A TRUE BOOK

Geology
The Study of Rocks

SUSAN H. GRAY

Children's Press®
An Imprint of Scholastic Inc.
New York Toronto London Auckland Sydney
Mexico City New Delhi Hong Kong
Danbury, Connecticut

Content Consultant
Pete Stelling, PhD
Assistant Professor, Geology Department
Western Washington University
Bellingham, Washington

Library of Congress Cataloging-in-Publication Data
Gray, Susan Heinrichs.
  Geology the study of rocks/by Susan H. Gray.
     p. cm.—(A true book)
  Includes bibliographical references and index.
  ISBN-13: 978-0-531-24676-4 (lib. bdg.)   ISBN-10: 0-531-24676-0 (lib. bdg.)
  ISBN-13: 978-0-531-28270-0 (pbk.)   ISBN-10: 0-531-28270-8 (pbk.)
  1. Geology—Juvenile literature. I. Title. II. Series.
  QE29.G73 2012
  551—dc23   2011031091

All rights reserved. Published in 2012 by Children's Press, an imprint of Scholastic Inc.
Printed in the United States of America 40
SCHOLASTIC, CHILDREN'S PRESS, A TRUE BOOK, and associated logos are trademarks and/or registered trademarks of Scholastic Inc.
          18 19 20 21 22 23 24 R 28 27 26 25 24 23

Find the Truth!

Everything you are about to read is true *except* for one of the sentences on this page.

Which one is **TRUE**?

T or F The earth's core is composed of slow-moving plates.

T or F The island of Iceland is growing.

Find the answers in this book.

3

Contents

THE **BIG** TRUTH!

Making Mountains Can Be Fast or Slow

Geologists look at different rock layers to understand the earth's history.

5

We can learn a lot
about the earth by
studying rocks.

Studying the Earth

Have you ever wondered about the earth you stand on every day? Some places are rugged, with mountains reaching above the clouds. Others are flat as far as the eye can see. Deep canyons cut through the land. Winding caves create mazes far below the surface. How and why are these things created? What exactly is the earth made of? Geologists ask questions like these every day.

Young people often go to geology camp to learn about rocks.

The Many Sides of Geology

Some geologists study the materials that make up the earth. They learn about the thousands of **minerals** found on the planet and how they are made. Some study the **fossils** that appear in rocks. Other geologists look at major structures on the earth's surface, such as mountains, plains, and riverbeds. They figure out how rain can wear down a mountain and how solid materials wash into the ocean. Some geologists even study how these processes might work on other planets.

High-pressure apparatus like this one help scientists mimic the pressures that exist deep in the Earth.

Volcanologists work closely with hot lava and other dangerous materials.

Seismologists and volcanologists watch for rapid changes in the earth. Seismologists keep track of earthquakes to learn why and how they occur. Volcanologists study volcanoes to understand what makes volcanoes erupt.

Some geologists look for energy sources. These include oil, natural gas, coal, and areas with **geothermal** activity. Other geologists look for areas where the rocks are strong and solid. They tell builders that these are the safest places to construct bridges, roads, and buildings.

The earth's mountains and valleys have changed shape slowly over millions of years.

CHAPTER 2

History of Geology

For thousands of years, scientists have wondered about the earth's mysteries. Why are there different layers of rock? How were mountain ranges and deep canyons formed? How old is the earth? Over the years, many people thought up creative explanations based on their observations. Often, when they told others their new ideas, no one believed them.

Canyons allow geologists to study many different rock layers.

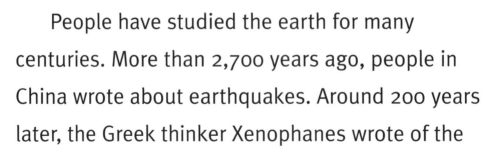

People have studied the earth for many centuries. More than 2,700 years ago, people in China wrote about earthquakes. Around 200 years later, the Greek thinker Xenophanes wrote of the fossils he found embedded in rocks. Another Greek, Aristotle, wrote about earthquakes and volcanoes. He believed they were caused by hot winds moving deep inside the earth.

Aristotle made many important contributions to science.

Minerals and Rocks

What exactly are minerals and rocks? Minerals
are solid materials that have a definite chemical
makeup. Some minerals are composed of just one
element, such as copper or silver. Others are made
of several elements that are chemically combined.
Rocks, however, are made up of different kinds of
materials—broken crystals, minerals, and even the
shells and skeletons of long-dead animals.

New Discoveries

In the 1700s, Scottish scientist James Hutton studied different layers of rocks. He noticed how rocks were worn down and shaped by wind and water. Hutton also saw that **sediment** from rocks and soil collected in layers. These observations led him to believe that very slow processes shaped landforms. Mountains were worn down and the seafloor built up over extremely long periods of time. Hutton believed that these processes created all the earth's rocks.

Timeline of Discoveries in Geology

About 350 BCE
Aristotle proposes the cause of earthquakes and volcanoes.

1788 CE
James Hutton introduces the idea of a rock cycle.

When Hutton shared his ideas with other scientists, they thought he had lost his mind. At the time, most people believed that the earth was around 6,000 years old. But if Hutton's idea was true, the earth had to be millions or even billions of years old. As time went on, more scientists found evidence that supported Hutton's observations. Today, his ideas are an important part of our understanding of the earth.

1840
Louis Agassiz publishes his ideas about glaciers.

1960s
Scientists develop the theory of the earth being divided into large slabs called plates.

The Aletsch Glacier caused the long scratches on this rock in Switzerland.

Louis Agassiz presented his own ideas about 50 years after Hutton. Agassiz was a Swiss scientist who believed that much of Europe had once been covered with glaciers.

Agassiz had noticed huge scratches and smooth spots on rocks. He believed that glaciers caused these marks as they slowly scraped across the landscape many years earlier. Like Hutton, Agassiz was criticized at first. As other scientists studied Agassiz's theories, his ideas gained acceptance.

In 1912, German scientist Alfred Wegener claimed that the earth's continents were once joined together. Over millions of years, they drifted apart. He called this process continental drift.

Some scientists ridiculed Wegener. They believed that continents were fixed in place. However, other scientists found evidence that the continents moved. Wegener's theory was found to be incorrect in many ways. But his ideas formed a basis for today's theory of **plate tectonics**, or shifting plates.

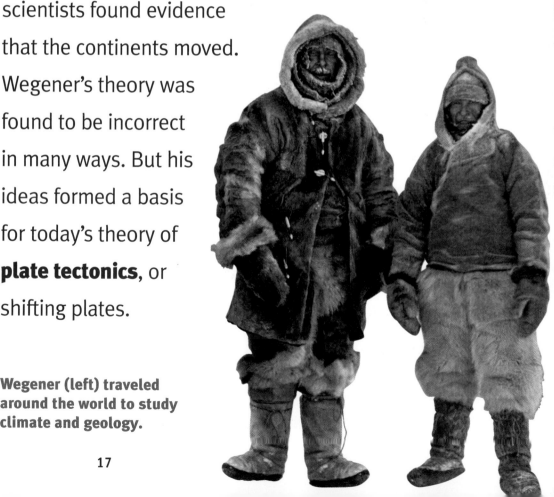

Wegener (left) traveled around the world to study climate and geology.

Volcanic eruptions can quickly cause major changes to the earth's surface.

CHAPTER 3

Our Rapidly and Slowly Changing Earth

Hutton, Agassiz, Wegener, and other geologists had one thing in common. They all believed that the earth was constantly changing. Geologists today agree that the earth, its rock layers, and its landforms do change very slowly. But there are also sudden, dramatic events that change things very quickly. Before we learn about those changes, we need to know about the earth's layers.

The word *volcano* comes from Vulcan, the Roman god of fire.

The earth can be divided into three main parts. These parts can be compared to the layers of a peach. The outer layer is called the crust. It is very thin, much like the skin of a peach. The continents, mountain ranges, and ocean floor are part of this layer. The crust is thinnest at the ocean floor. There, it is about 5 miles (8 kilometers) thick. It is thickest where landmasses rise above ocean level. There, it averages about 30 miles (48 km) in depth.

Some geologists study the ocean floor.

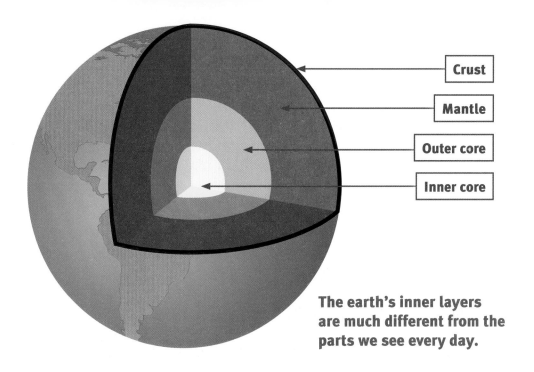

Crust

Mantle

Outer core

Inner core

The earth's inner layers are much different from the parts we see every day.

The mantle is beneath the crust. Like the fleshy part of the peach, it is very thick. The mantle extends for about 1,800 miles (2,900 km). It is made up of very dense rock. Long ago, people thought that the crust and mantle did not move. But scientists now agree that the crust and some of the upper mantle are actually in constant motion.

Deepest of all is the earth's core. This is like the peach's pit. The core's outer portion is liquid metal. Its center is a solid ball mostly of iron and nickel.

This deep underwater canyon was created by two plates moving away from each other.

The Earth's Slow Changes

How can the entire crust stay in constant motion? It is divided into several enormous slabs. These slabs—or tectonic plates—scoot around. They bump into each other. They move away from each other and grind alongside each other. Some plates even slide under the edges of other plates. These movements are extremely slow. They are detected only with special instruments.

Plate movements can produce incredible results. The collision of two plates millions of years ago caused the earth to buckle in Asia. The ground rose up, forming the Himalayas.

Iceland straddles two plates that are moving apart. Cracks have formed in the ground in some areas. The cracks grow larger every month. These cracks force Iceland itself to expand. Today, the island expands almost 1 inch (2.54 centimeters) each year.

Volcanic activity is common along the Mid-Atlantic Ridge in Iceland.

Plate boundaries are areas of intense heat.

Erosion is another slow process that changes the earth. This is the process in which nature removes soil and rock from one place and deposits them in a different place. A seaside cliff shows the effects of erosion. As the sea's waves beat against the cliff, they knock off rock particles. These wash into the water and sink. They become part of the sediment on the seafloor. As the cliff wears away, the seafloor slowly builds up.

Erosion creates interesting cliffs along coastlines.

River and stream banks are eroded by the flowing water every day.

Soil, sand, and rocks travel through streams to reach larger bodies of water.

Wind, ice, and rain also slowly erode landforms. Strong winds can move soil and pebbles down a mountainside. Constant exposure to water can soften rocks. This allows them to break into smaller pieces more easily. Water that freezes in the cracks of a rock can break the rock into smaller pieces. Rainstorms can carry these pieces off to settle in streambeds.

Making Mountains Can Be Fast or Slow

Mountains can be pushed up gradually by the slow collision of plates. They can also be formed by rapid events such as volcanoes. Erosion creates mountains as well. The Ozarks of Missouri and Arkansas were formed this way. Long ago, the area was under the ocean. Sediment steadily gathered, thickening the crust. Over time, the land rose up, exposed as a high, mostly flat plain. Erosion slowly carved this broad landmass into mountains and valleys.

The Himalayas lie along the northern part of India. They slowly rose up as plates collided. These plates are still colliding today. As a result, the mountains are increasing in height each year.

The Hawaiian Islands were created by volcanoes. Some of those volcanoes are still active today. Geologists keep track of their activities. They even post their photographs and videos on the Internet. In some places, tourists can also visit the volcanoes.

The Ozarks are mostly low, rounded hills. In many places, erosion has exposed fossils. These fossils are the remains of ocean plants and animals. They were deposited there when the land was underwater.

The largest tsunamis can be taller than a 10-story building.

A 2011 tsunami caused massive destruction in Japan.

Rapid Changes

Not all changes to the earth are slow. Earthquakes occur rapidly. They take place when two tectonic plates rub against each other. The edge of one plate becomes hung up, then suddenly comes unstuck. This causes a jolt that can be felt far above on the earth's surface.

Earthquakes that occur beneath the ocean can set off enormous ocean waves called **tsunamis**. These powerful and fast-moving waves can be quite destructive to coastal areas.

The shifting of plates also creates volcanoes. A volcano is an opening in the crust. It allows ash, gas, and molten rock from the mantle to flow through to the earth's surface. In some eruptions, these materials burst forth in an explosion. Volcanic ash is sent into the air and can be carried miles away by the wind. In other eruptions, lava simply oozes out and flows down the side of the volcano.

Some volcanic eruptions are more powerful than others.

CHAPTER 4

The Rock Cycle

The earth is constantly changing. Major events such as volcanoes and earthquakes and even erosion may seem random.

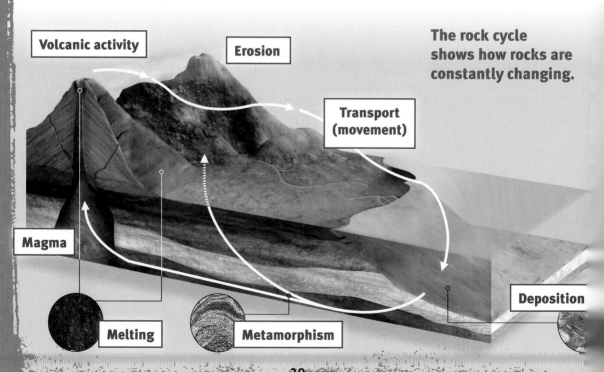

Volcanic activity

Erosion

The rock cycle shows how rocks are constantly changing.

Transport (movement)

Magma

Deposition

Melting

Metamorphism

These changes are all part of a pattern, however. This pattern is called the rock cycle. Rocks and minerals are created, destroyed, and renewed.

Some events in the cycle occur over millions of years. Other events, such as volcanic eruptions, occur quickly.

Geologists divide the rock cycle into three basic stages. Each stage creates a certain kind of rock: **igneous**, **sedimentary**, or **metamorphic**. The stages can be happening at the same time at different places on the earth.

James Hutton introduced the idea of the rock cycle more than 200 years ago.

Magma that reaches the earth's surface is called lava.

Magma cools quickly when it reaches the earth's surface.

Igneous Rocks

One stage in the rock cycle creates igneous rocks. Igneous rocks begin as **magma**.

In certain locations deep inside the earth, temperature and pressure are just right to melt rock into magma. Some magma travels to the surface through volcanoes. After escaping the volcano, the magma cools very quickly.

Some magma rises toward the earth's surface but cannot escape the crust. This magma cools and hardens anyway. Because it is not exposed to the cool air at the earth's surface, the process takes thousands of years.

Magma might harden quickly or slowly. Either way, hardened magma becomes solid igneous rock.

Most igneous rock forms underground, but some forms on the surface.

Settling Into Sedimentary Rock

As plates collide, some rocks are pushed up into mountains. At the same time, erosion wears down those mountains. Erosion also wears down volcanoes and igneous rocks. Wind and rain carry the soil and rock particles away. They are deposited into valleys, onto lake beds, and on the ocean floor.

Limestone and sandstone are two examples of sedimentary rock.

Patterns of lines often develop in sedimentary rocks.

Erosion sometimes carves rocks into interesting shapes.

When eroded pieces of rock are moved to a low spot in the earth or ocean, they begin to pile up. This process is called **deposition**. Dead plants and animals might also pile up with the soil and rock particles. This layer of materials is called sediment. As more and more materials pile on, the weight presses the lower layers of sediment into solid rock. The solid material created in this stage is called sedimentary rock.

Metamorphic rocks are often extremely hard.

Metamorphic Rocks Under Pressure

As the sedimentary layers build up, the deepest ones come under intense pressure and heat. This can also happen to igneous rocks located deep beneath the earth's crust. The pressure and heat change the chemical makeup of these rocks. Their minerals are forced to change, or morph, into other kinds of minerals. As they change in this stage, they turn into metamorphic rocks. Heat and pressure can also change one kind of metamorphic rock into another.

The Rock Cycle Continues

Rocks caught between two colliding plates can sometimes be slowly pressed downward. As they move closer to the mantle, they experience more of the mantle's intense heat. They may also be involved in chemical reactions that occur only at plate boundaries. The heat and chemical reactions melt the rocks into magma. The magma collects, and some of it travels to the earth's surface. It cools and hardens into igneous rock, beginning the cycle again.

The word *igneous* comes from the Latin word for "fire."

The rock cycle ensures that the earth's surface will continue to change for as long as the planet exists.

Geologists travel around the world to collect information about different areas.

CHAPTER 5

Frozen Fields and Outer Space

Geologists do not always focus on the heat and pressure of plates, quakes, and volcanoes. Some geologists travel the Arctic and Antarctic. They explore these icy regions and make maps of places that no one else has ever studied. Their work often helps other scientists. For example, new maps and photographs of the area can help zoologists learn how polar animals survive.

Geologists gather samples in the field, but study them in the lab.

Space exploration has opened a new door in geology. Astronauts' trips to the moon in the 20th century were only the beginning. The Mars Rovers drive across the red planet to study rocks and soil. They send their data back to Earth. Satellites have sailed by all the planets in our solar system, beaming back pictures and other information. Astrogeologists use this information to create maps and descriptions of planets, moons, and other rocky objects in space. These geologists might someday help us know if there is life on other planets in our solar system.

Mars Rovers and other technology help scientists learn about the geology of other planets.

Geology to the Rescue

Years ago, Japan's government hired scientists to create an earthquake warning system. The system would notify everyone of a coming earthquake. The program began operating in 2007. In 2011, Japan suffered a tremendous quake. As rock deep inside the earth broke apart, shock waves traveled to the surface. Millions of people received text messages and e-mails warning them to take cover. The quake caused widespread damage and many deaths. But thanks to the warning system, countless lives were saved.

Geologists still have a lot to learn about the way our planet works.

Just like the earth, the science of geology is constantly changing. As our technology improves, geologists might someday discover a way to predict earthquakes and volcanoes years before they erupt. They might travel deep inside the earth to get a peek at the mantle. They may one day walk on Mars. Who knows what will be discovered in the coming years? ★

Size of the earth: About 25,000 mi. (40,234 km) around the equator

Deepest slice in the earth's crust: The Mariana Trench, a trench in the Pacific Ocean floor that goes down almost 7 mi. (11 km)

Highest mountain in the world as measured from sea level: Mount Everest in the Himalayas, which rises 29,035 ft. (8,850 m) above sea level

Highest mountain in the world as measured from the ocean floor: Mauna Loa, on Hawaii, which rises 56,000 ft. (17,069 m) from the base of the mountain on the ocean floor to its summit

What covers the earth: About 70 percent is covered by water and 30 percent is covered by land

Did you find the truth?

F The earth's core is composed of slow-moving plates.

T The island of Iceland is growing.

Resources

Books

Brown, Cynthia Light. *Geology of the Pacific Northwest: Investigate How the Earth Was Formed With 15 Projects*. Norwich, VT: Nomad Press, 2011.

Clifford, Tim. *Geology*. Vero Beach, FL: Rourke Publishing, 2008.

Faulkner, Rebecca. *Crystals*. Chicago: Raintree, 2007.

Faulkner, Rebecca. *Minerals*. Chicago: Raintree, 2007.

Petersen, Christine. *Mighty Minerals*. Edina, MN: ABDO Publishing Company, 2010.

Saunders, Craig. *What Is the Theory of Plate Tectonics?* New York: Crabtree Publishing, 2011.

Stiefel, Chana. *Tsunamis*. New York: Children's Press, 2009.

Van Rose, Susanna. *Volcano*. New York: DK Eyewitness Books, 2008.

Organizations and Web Sites

KidsGeo.com—Geology for Kids

www.kidsgeo.com/geology-for-kids

This site has plenty of basic information about geology.

U.S. Geological Survey

www.usgs.gov

Learn about floods, earthquakes, tsunamis, and more.

Places to Visit

Colorado School of Mines Geology Museum

General Research Laboratory (GRL) building
1310 Maple Street
Golden, CO 80401
(303) 273-3815
www.mines.edu/Geology_Museum
See many different samples of rocks and minerals, including rocks from the moon.

Natural History Museum of Los Angeles County

900 Exposition Boulevard
Los Angeles, CA 90007
(213) 763-3466
www.nhm.org/site
This museum features a permanent exhibit with more than 2,000 gemstones.

 Visit this Scholastic web site for more information on geology:
www.factsfornow.scholastic.com

Important Words

deposition (deh-puh-ZIH-shuhn) — the process in which sediments collect in a certain place

element (EL-uh-muhnt) — a basic substance containing only one kind of atom

fossils (FAH-suhlz) — remains of ancient life

geothermal (jee-oh-THER-muhl) — related to the heat generated in the earth's interior

igneous (IG-nee-uhss) — resulting from volcanic activity

magma (MAG-muh) — molten rock material within the earth

metamorphic (met-uh-MOR-fik) — relating to something that has undergone a change in form or structure

minerals (MIN-ur-uhlz) — naturally occurring substances obtained from the ground

plate tectonics (PLAYT tek-TAHN-iks) — the theory that the earth's crust is divided into several large plates

sediment (SED-uh-muhnt) — material deposited by water, wind, or glaciers

sedimentary (sed-uh-MEN-tuh-ree) — rock formed by layers of sediment in the ground being pressed together

tsunamis (tsu-NAH-meez) — great sea waves caused by underwater earthquakes

Index

Page numbers in **bold** indicate illustrations

About the Author

Susan H. Gray has a master's degree in zoology and has also studied geology and paleontology. She has written more than 120 reference books for children. Susan especially likes to write on topics that engage children in science. She and her husband, Michael, live in Cabot, Arkansas.